LEARN WITH TUNES

A Melodic Approach to the Violin for Individual or Class Instruction

by CARL GRISSEN

ISBN 978-1-70516-065-7

I0806887

WILLIS MUSIC

EXCLUSIVELY DISTRIBUTED BY

HAL•LEONARD®

Visit Hal Leonard Online at
www.halleonard.com

Contact us:
Hal Leonard
7777 West Bluemound Road
Milwaukee, WI 53213
Email: info@halleonard.com

In Europe, contact:
Hal Leonard Europe Limited
42 Wigmore Street
Marylebone, London, W1U 2RN
Email: info@halleonardeurope.com

In Australia, contact:
Hal Leonard Australia Pty. Ltd.
4 Lentara Court
Cheltenham, Victoria, 3192 Australia
Email: info@halleonard.com.au

PREFACE

The primary objective of the pupil is to derive pleasure from his study of the violin. The tonal sequences of a pretty tune are much more to his liking than the so-called dry scales and exercises, and if his idealistic concept of music is not to be rudely shocked there must be a judicious and logical balancing of the one element against the other.

In addition to the original melodic material in Books I and II, designed with especial reference to the problems in each lesson, there is a generous inclusion of old favorites for solo, duet, and ensemble playing, which, at once serve as musical landmarks to the pupil, and media for the exploitation of technical problems in their proper time and place.

In beginning stopped tones it may be observed that pupils often have their minds centered upon playing a *note* rather than the exact *tone* that the note represents. Do-Re intoned by the pupil represents a definite tonal concept of what is required. A-B in printed notes does not—as yet. If the first progressions are sol-faed correctly before they are played, the printed note is transformed into a tonal symbol; a definite intention takes the place of indefinite groping. For this reason the Sol-fa syllables have been added to some of the lessons to simplify the work of both teacher and pupil.

New rhythmical problems are first presented on the open strings in order that the attention may be concentrated on bow control free from left hand interference. New rhythm patterns should be thoroughly understood by counting, la-ing and tapping, playing the figure without music, and at last playing from the music while counting aloud.

The element of expression, elaborated according to the fancy of the teacher, is important in that it awakens the imagination and gives impetus to greater effort. The lesson-hour should be an inspirational experience rather than a monotonous incident in the weekly routine.

The standards set by the teacher will bear fruit accordingly; if a high degree of excellence is demanded in regard to the three vital T's of good violin playing: TUNE, TONE and TIME, the pupil will try to measure up to the requirements of his teacher.

Carl Grissen

THE A-B-C OF MUSIC

The Notes used in music are symbols of Sound.

These sounds may be high or low, short or long, according to their position upon the Staff and their Time value.

The notes are written upon, above, or below the staff.

The staff consists of five lines and four spaces, numbered upwards.

The Staff: 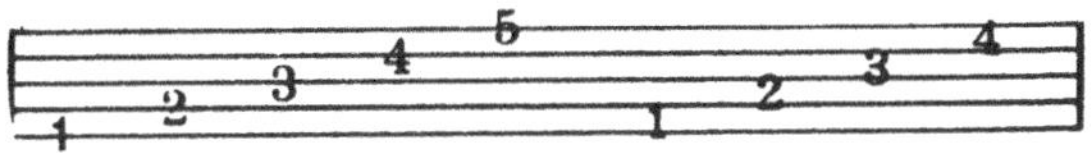

A sign called the G Clef is placed at the beginning of the staff.

The lower part of the clef curls around the second line of the staff, fixing the name of that line as G.

The G Clef: 

The music is divided into Measures of equal time value by placing a vertical line called a Bar at intervals across the staff.

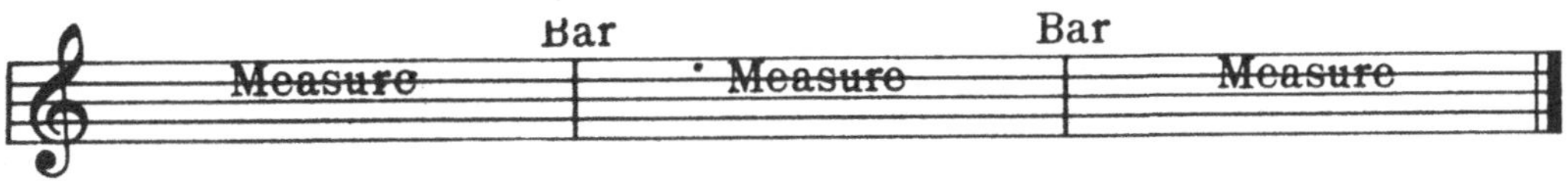

The Time Signature is a fraction placed at the beginning of the music; it shows the number of Counts or Beats in each measure, and the value of a note that gets a count. The upper figure shows the number of counts in a measure; the lower figure determines the value of the note that equals one count or beat. In $\frac{4}{4}$ time, four counts are required to the measure; quarter notes get one count each.

Examples of different kinds of time with the quarter note as the unit of measurement.

Whole Note=Two Half Notes=Four Quarter Notes = Eight Eighth Notes.

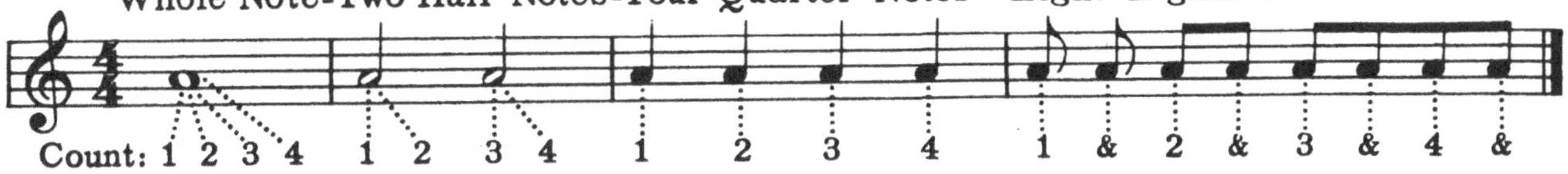

Dotted Half Note = Three Quarter Notes = Six Eighth Notes.

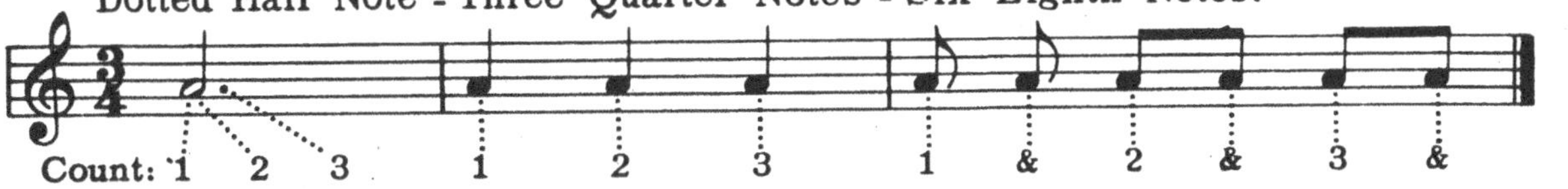

Examples of Time with the Eighth Note as the unit of measurement; singly, an eighth note is written thus: ; two or more are attached to a Beam .

4 = four beats to the measure.
In $\frac{4}{8}$ time 8 = eighth notes get one count each.

Half Note=Two Quarter Notes=Four Eighth Notes = Eight Sixteenth Notes.

Rests mean that the player pauses or is silent for as many counts as the rest calls for. Rests have their value the same as notes.

The letters of the alphabet, A, B, C, D, E, F, G, are used to name the notes in music. Each line and space of the staff counts for one degree.

Ledger Lines are used to write notes higher or lower than those on the staff.

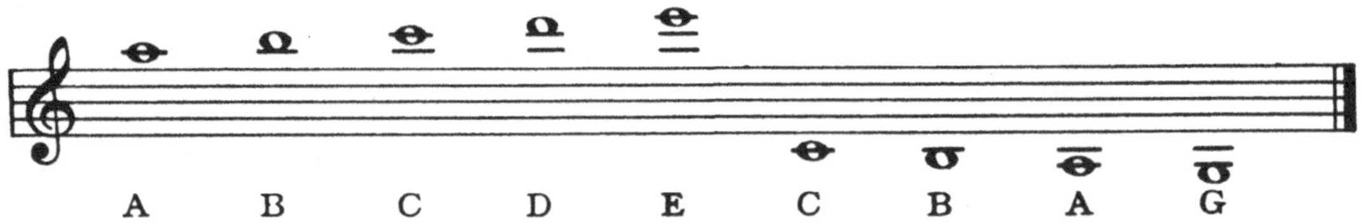

To remember the names of the lines and the spaces:

A light Double Bar ‖ marks a division, and a heavy Double Bar, ‖ the end of a piece.

Two Dots before a double bar mean to repeat that part.

Repeat Sign: 

SHARPS, FLATS, NATURALS

A Sharp (♯) raises a note one-half tone.

A Flat (♭) lowers a note one-half tone.

A Natural (♮) cancels a sharp or a flat; the note then becomes the same as it was before it was sharped or flatted.

All music is written in certain Keys. The sharps or flats that are placed on the staff to the right of the clef sign form the Key Signature. Here we have the key signature of D Major.

The first sharp is on the fifth line; the name of this line is F—therefore this is F sharp—it sharps all F's. The second sharp is on the third space which makes it C sharp.

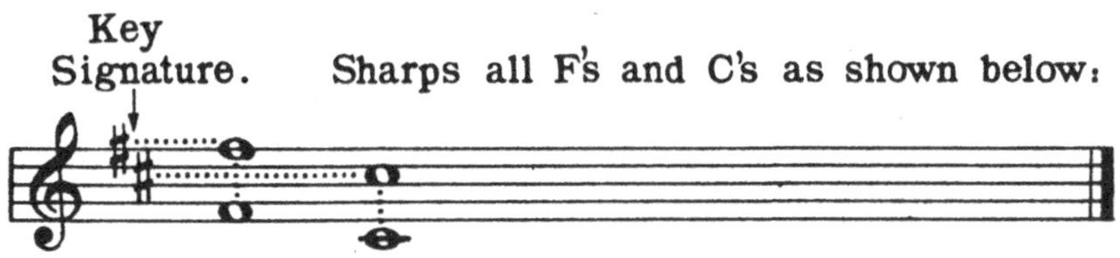

PARTS OF THE VIOLIN

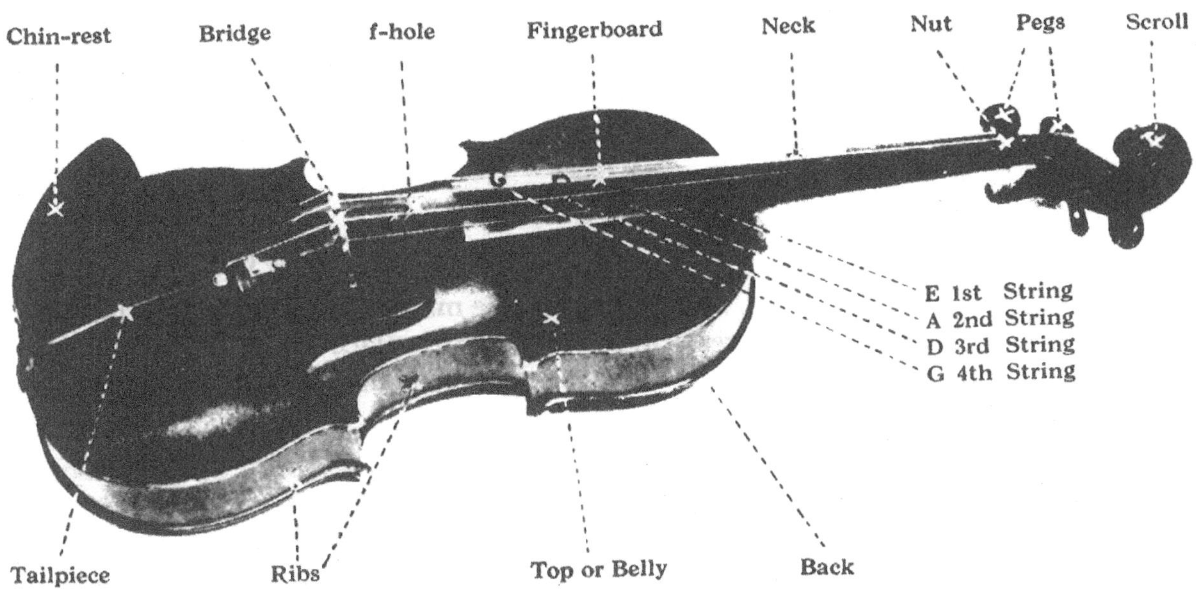

It is important for the pupil to have a violin of the proper size for his age.

The table below is an approximation of average requirements.

Age	Size of Violin	Age	Size of Violin
4 to 5 yrs.	1/8	7 to 9 yrs.	1/2
5 to 6 yrs.	1/4	9 to 12 yrs.	3/4
13 years upward			Full size

HOW TO HOLD THE VIOLIN

The violin should be equipped with chin-rest, shoulder pad, and E string adjuster.

Do not hold the bow at first; the right hand is needed to secure the violin in learning the right position.

1. Place the lower edge of the violin upon the collar-bone, the chin upon the chin-rest. Hold the head straight.

2. Swing the left elbow well to the right; an imaginary line dropped from the center of the instrument should strike the elbow-joint. The scroll should be in line with the left shoulder.

3. Maintain a high chest position.

4. Bring the left hand to the violin neck which should rest between the base of the first finger and the end joint of the thumb; the position of the thumb is about one inch from the nut with not more than one-half inch of the end joint visible above the fingerboard. The violin neck must not fall into the lower crotch between thumb and hand. The thumb should be held straight and not clinch the neck.

5. Curve the fingers over the strings with the left palm at a narrow angle from the fingerboard—close enough that the little finger will always be above the strings. The middle knuckle of the first finger to the elbow should describe a nearly straight line.

6. The chin and the left shoulder should mostly support the instrument, thus giving more freedom to the left hand.

7. Most violinists of the present day use the so called "spraddle position", standing evenly on both feet placed about one foot apart.

HOW TO HOLD THE BOW

Secure the bow with the left hand six inches from the frog, the hair down:

1. Bend the right thumb upward, its tip opposite the middle finger, the right hand and forearm in horizontal position with the fingers curved downward; place the tip of the thumb at the juncture of the frog and the stick. Do not push the thumb all the way into the curved space of the frog.

2. Place the fingers over the stick: (a) the first finger pressed lightly upon the stick at the beginning of the third joint (Russian manner), the first and second joints curved and touching the stick; (b) the second finger contacts the stick at the second joint; (c) the third finger contacts just below the first joint; (d) the little finger is curved with its tip resting upon the stick. In practical use the little finger may fall away from the stick on the down bow after passing the middle, but is indispensable as a counterbalance from the middle to the frog in the up bow.

3. The fingers curve in a natural, relaxed manner and are not pressed together. The ends of the second and third fingers touch the side of the frog, and the thumb is opposite the second finger.

4. Practice taking up the bow until you can hold it with an easy, relaxed hand, without clutching.

POSITION OF THE BOW UPON THE STRINGS

Place the violin and the bow in playing position and study the illustrations.

1. The bow should be tilted slightly by inclining the stick toward the fingerboard.

2. The hair contacts the strings a trifle over one inch from the bridge.

3. The bow must always be drawn parallel with the bridge, and forms a right angle to the strings.

4. When the bow is at the point the wrist bends slightly. When at the frog there is a slight inclination upward.

5. In the beginning it is most important to work for relaxation of the whole bow arm, concentrating upon the movements of hand, forearm and arm.

HOW TO TUNE THE VIOLIN

1. Beginners should have a pitch-pipe that sounds the pitch of each string. Blow the tones softly to get a pure tone.

2. The wire E strings now in use are non-elastic and difficult to tune by means of the peg alone; having an E string adjuster affixed to the tail-piece simplifies the tuning of this string.

3. It is important to practice with your instrument always tuned to standard pitch. Your pitch-pipe or the tones on a well-tuned piano.

4. Beginners should first tune by placing the lower part of the violin between the knees while seated.

5. First tune the A string to pitch with the right hand. The D and G strings are then tuned in turn with the left hand. The E string is tuned last; it is first brought to pitch by using the peg—after that the E tuner will do the work of keeping this string in tune.

6. While tuning with one hand brace the violin with the other using the free thumb to pluck and sound the string that is being tuned. The A and E pegs are turned with the right hand, the D and G with the left.

7. Always press the pegs inward as you turn them that they will not slip when the string is brought to pitch. The knack of tuning the instrument in playing position will come in due time.

8. The ear can soon be trained to accurate tuning in the following manner: tune the A to the pitch-pipe, then sing:

(1)

sol fa mi re do = D–3rd string.

Tune the G in the same manner.

(2)

sol fa mi re do = G–4th string.

(3)

The E is then tuned, do re mi fa sol = E–1st string.

THE CARE OF THE VIOLIN AND THE BOW

1. A new bow requires a thorough application of powdered and solid rosin before using; thereafter a few strokes of rosin to the hair before each practice period is sufficient.

2. To retain the elasticity of the bow-stick loosen the hair until it almost touches the stick when not in use. After using wipe off all accumulated rosin dust from the stick. If the bow-hair becomes soiled at the frog it can be washed with soap and warm water by removing the bow-screw and lifting out the frog.

3. Daily remove the rosin dust from between the bridge and the end of the fingerboard; if left uncared for, rosin and dust soon form a gummy mass difficult to clean and injurious to tone.

4. Use only first class strings—cheap strings are generally false. Always keep an extra set on hand.

5. Before attempting to use a long neglected violin have it thoroughly adjusted by a competent violin maker.

6. After using put the instrument away in its case; keep free from dampness.

7. In the course of time, tuning pulls the bridge top forward; watch this or it may fall and split.

Bow at the middle.

The violin is properly placed on the collar bone, and the shoulders are in normal position.

Bow near the point at right-angles to the strings.

The left elbow, swung well to the right, can be seen by the right eye of the player.

The chin and the neck are relaxed, and the scroll of the violin is tilted slightly upward.

Bow at the frog or nut.

Note the co-ordination of arm, forearm and hand forming a relaxed bow-arm. The bow stick tilts toward the fingerboard.

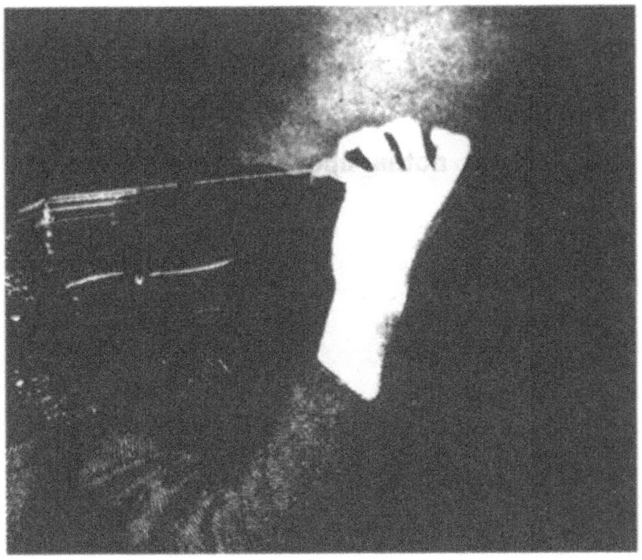

Left hand in the first position.

The third joint of the first finger, the hand and the forearm form a straight line; the palm of the hand is held close enough to the violin neck so that the fourth finger will always be in playing position above the strings.

Only the finger tips contact the strings.

Front View.

Showing a faulty position of the fingers on the bow, and a high awkward position of the right arm.

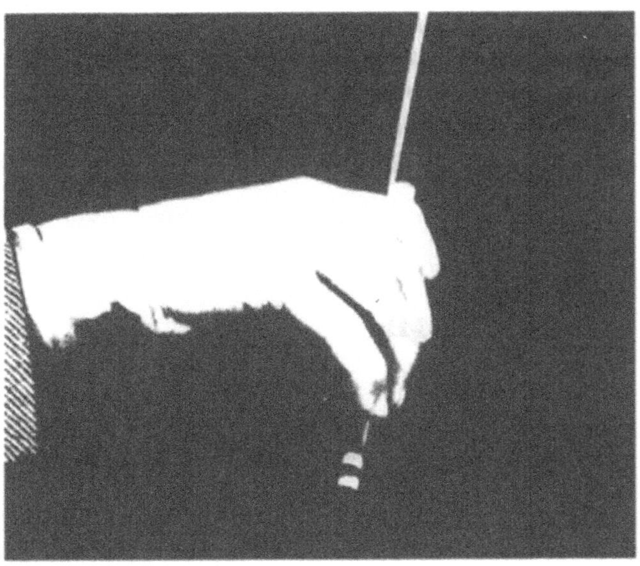

Position of the fingers upon the bow.

Note the individual placement of each finger. The first finger contacts the bow at the beginning of the third joint, and curving around the stick touches it at the first and second joints.

The tip of the curved fourth finger rests upon the bow.

Position of the thumb upon the bow.

Each joint is bent, and the tip contacts both frog and stick opposite the second finger; a stiff, straight thumb stiffens the entire hand.

LESSON 1
The Open Strings

Diagram of the open strings, and the open string notes upon the staff

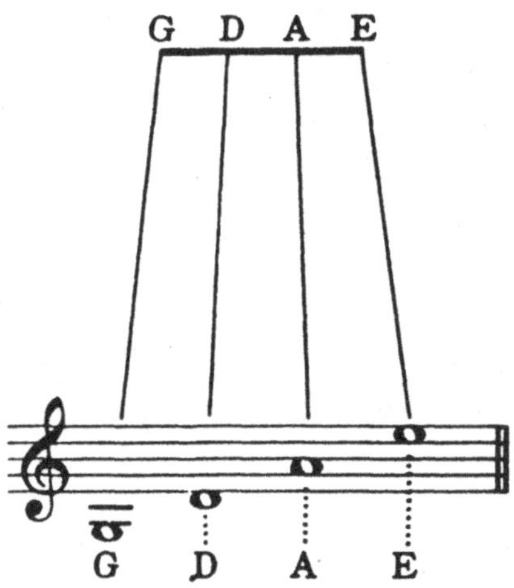

How to practice this lesson:

The quarter notes and quarter rests each get one count.

1. First recite the exercise as follows:

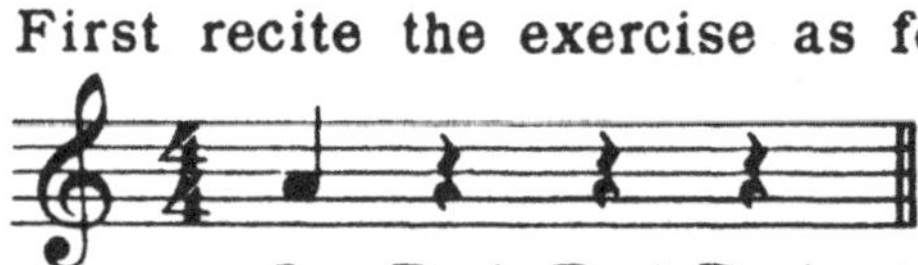

La, Rest, Rest, Rest, *etc.*

2. Now play the exercise without looking at the music;
   (a) watch the position of the bow—draw it straight;
   (b) keep the bow on the strings during the rests;
   (c) relax the hand and bow arm while counting the rests.
3. Play from the music while counting aloud, 1, 2, 3, 4.

The Open A String

Use a few inches of bow in the middle

⊓ Sign for Down Bow
V Up Bow

1. 

Count: 1 2 3 4 1 2 3 4

The Open D String

2. 

Count: 1 2 3 4

3. 

Count: 1 2 3 4

Another sign for 4/4 time.
4.
During the rests tip the bow to the next required string without lifting.
5.
Count: 1 2 3 4
6.
7.
8.
9.
Count: 1 2 3 4 1 2 3 4
10.
11.
Count: 1 2 3 4
Little Duet
C. G.
Pupil
12.
Teacher

LESSON 2

The Open D and G Strings

Half Notes and Half Measure Rests

1. Recite No.-1:
2. Play the exercise observing the bow position, and relaxing the right hand and arm.
3. Play from the music counting aloud.
4. Draw the bow lightly over the strings.
5. Keep the bow on the strings during the rests.
6. During the rests tip the bow onto the next required string

Use the Middle Third of the Bow.

1. 

Count: 1 2 3 4

2. 

3. 

4.

5.

Count: 1 2 3 4

6.

Count: 1 2 3 4

Hand in Hand

C. G.

7.

Evening Song

C. G.

8.

LESSON 3

The open E and A strings using quarter notes and half notes without rests

1. Play No. 1 in medium tempo to form the concept of a free, flowing tone.
2. On the E string the bow arm drops a little lower toward the body.
3. Use less bow for the quarter notes, more bow for the half notes.
4. Practice the exercises slowly at first, with enough bow to produce a free, flowing tone, then a little faster, using less bow.
5. Good *time* and proper *accentuation* make for good *rhythm,* the life-pulse of music.
6. The accents in $\frac{2}{4}$ and $\frac{4}{4}$ are:

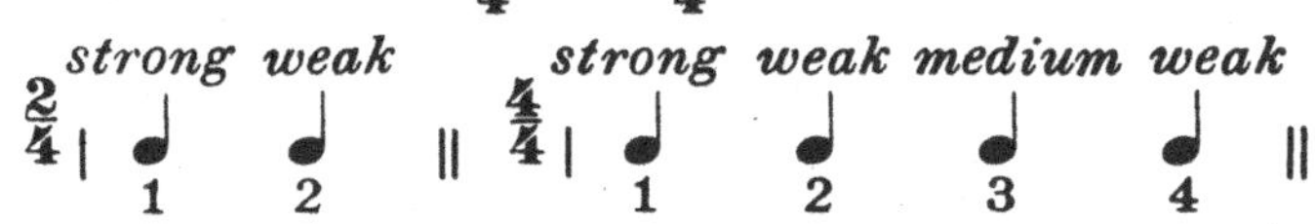

The Open E String

1. 

2. 

3. 

4. 

Sunset

C.G.

$\frac{2}{4}$ Time: Two counts to the measure.

To Market

C. G.

The Fox and the Goose

German Folk Song

LESSON 4

Whole Notes–Whole Rests

How to practice this lesson

1. In using the whole bow several movements of the hand, forearm and arm are synchronized for the first time. For several weeks the use of the whole bow should be limited in bow length from the Nut to about six inches from the Point; farther extension of the bow will come naturally and without cramping.
2. Starting at the Nut, down bow, the arm from the shoulder to elbow moves first until approximately the middle of the bow is reached, then the forearm finishes the stroke, the wrist sinking in slightly. The up bow is just the reverse of this.
3. Understand the counting of Whole Notes and Whole Rests, then practice No. 1, observing the movements of the hand, forearm and arm; move the bow straight with the bridge, and relax the arm while counting the whole rests. Use no pressure and save the bow on the whole notes.

Keep bow on string during rests

5.

6.

7.

8.

9.

10.

Skirlin' the Pipes

C. G.

Allegretto (Medium fast)

11.

U.H. Upper Half
L.H. Lower Half
Fr. at Frog
W.B. Whole Bow
Pt. Point

LESSON 5

Division of the Bow

1. 

2. 

Always look ahead for what is coming in the next measure.

3. 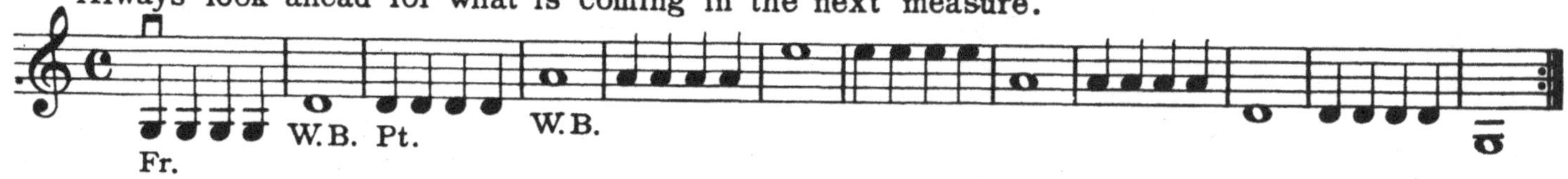

4. 

5. 

6. 

Onward, Christian Soldiers

Sullivan

7. 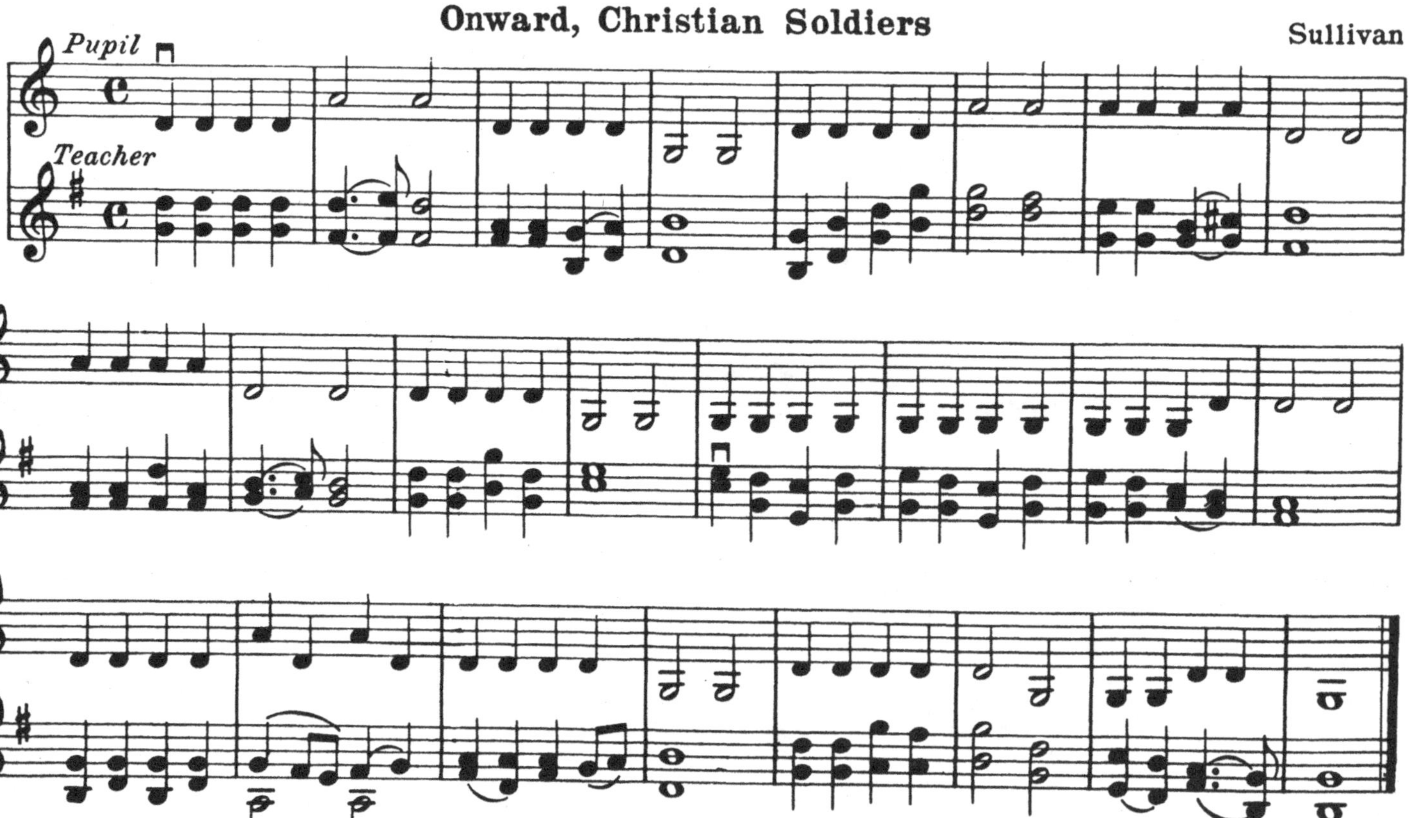

LESSON 6

Eighth Notes – Eighth Rests

An eighth note (♪). Eighth rest (𝄾). Two eighths (♫) = a quarter note.

Jingle Bells

J. Pierpont

May Morning

C. G.

LESSON 7

The First Finger on the A string

The first finger tone on the A string is B; to get this tone well in mind sing Do, Re from the pitch of the open A string.

1. 

3. 

5. 

Progress

7. 

The First Finger on the D string

The first finger tone on the D string is E. Proceed as in No. 1

8. 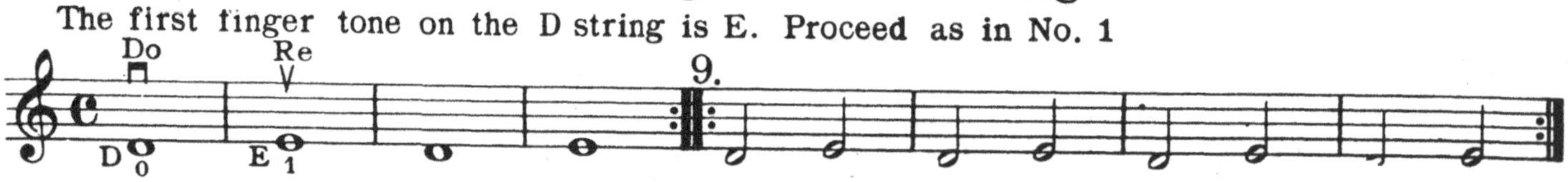

Keep the fingers curved over the strings and the third joint of the first finger in a straight line with the hand.

10. 

Move the first finger *straight* across the strings; do not bend back or forward.

12. 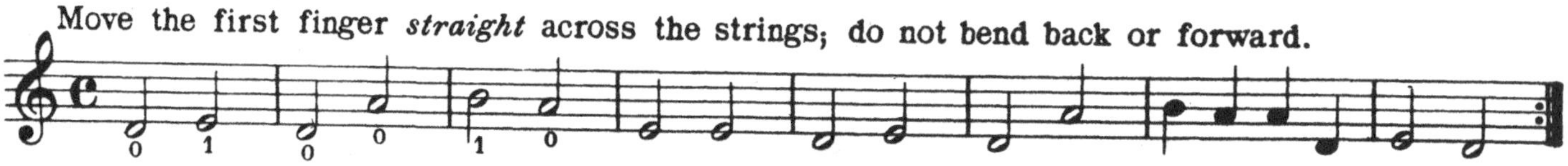

Four O'clock

C. G.

13. 

LESSON 8

First Finger on the E, A, D, G Strings

First finger plays F♯ on the E string.

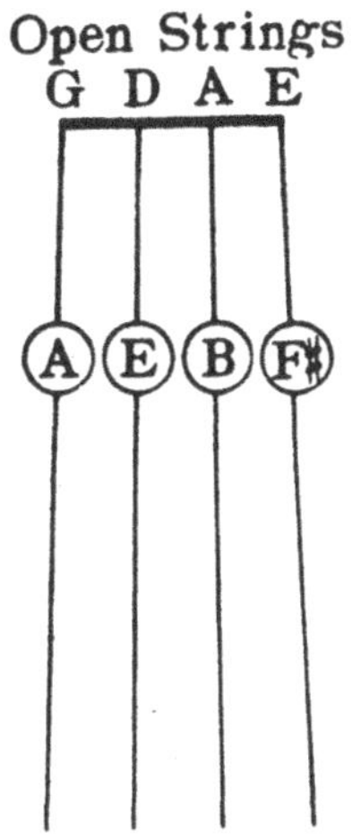

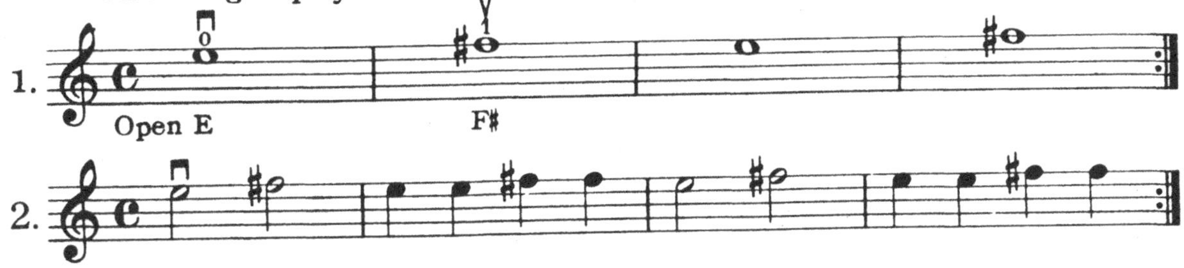

First finger tones straight across on all strings – a whole tone from the nut.

First finger plays A on the G string.

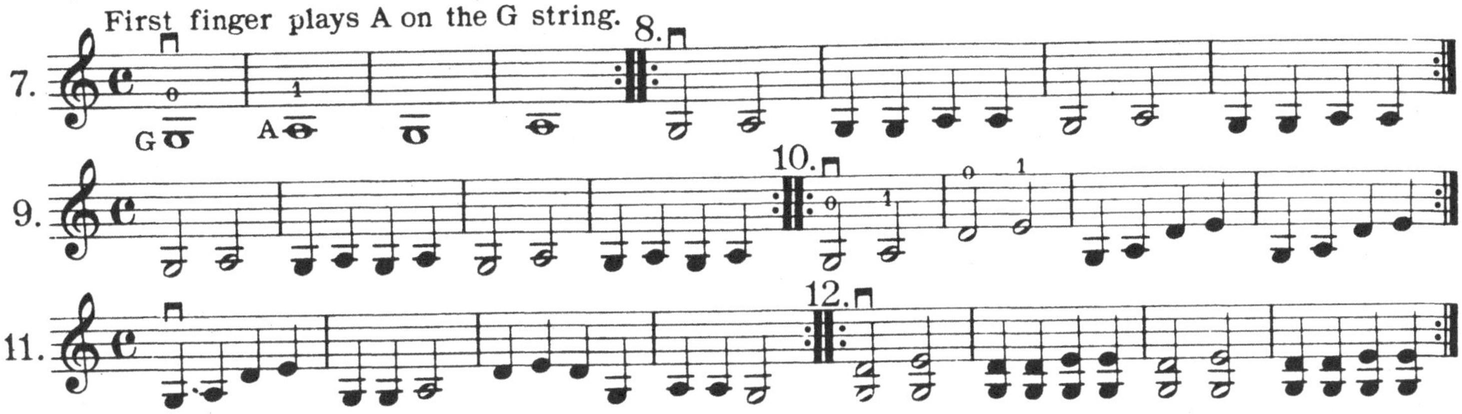

A Musical Puzzle

C. G.

Tune of the First Finger

C. G.

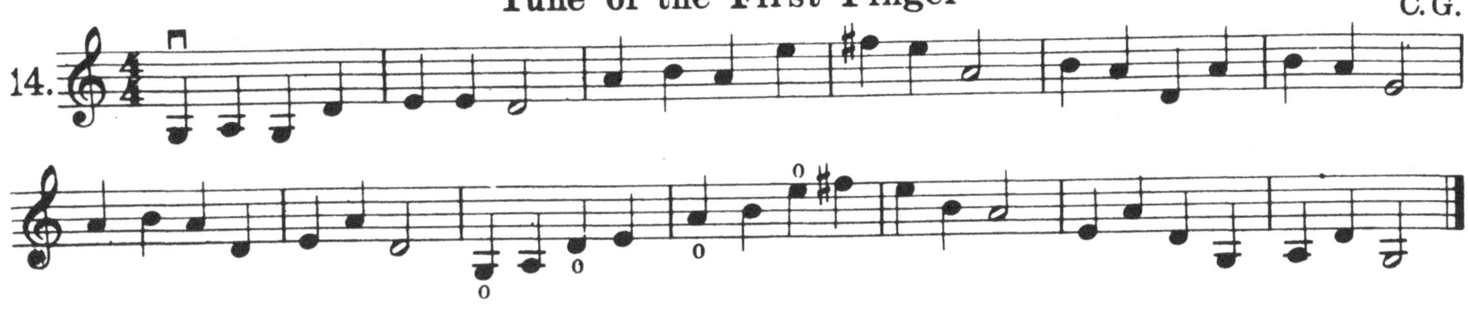

LESSON 9

The 1st, 2nd and 3rd Fingers on the A String

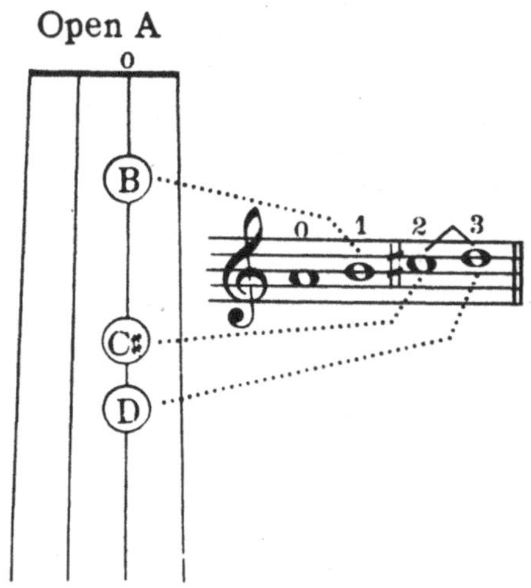

Sign for Half Tone–fingers close together.

1. 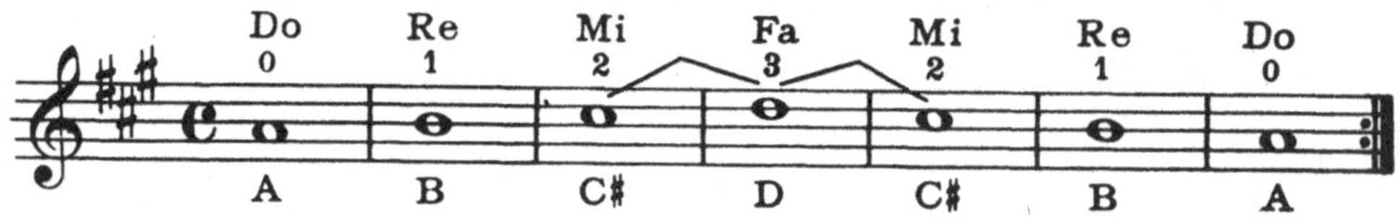

Keep the fingers down on the string wherever possible.

2. 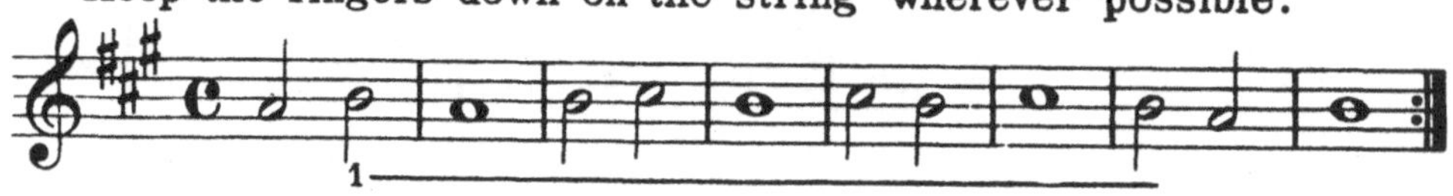

Note the Key Signature of three sharps: F♯, C♯, G♯; the key is A major: all C's are *sharped*.

3. 

4. 

6. 

8. 

9. 

Forward March

C. G.

10. 

Little Dance

C.G.

11. 

The Slur

When two or more notes are to be played in one bow, a curved line called a Slur is placed above or below the notes. A slur: ⁀

12. 

13. 

14. 

Heads Up March

C.G.

15. 

*Here the curved line is called a Tie; two notes of the same pitch tied together for three counts without a break.

For Written Work

Write the following words on the staff using whole notes: Place a double bar between each word.

Example: A C E : A G E D : B E D : B A G D A D : B A G G A G E :

C A G E : C A F E : C A B B A G E : C A D : C E D E : D A B :

D E A F : F A D : F E D : F A G : G A G E : G A B : G A D :

Hints on Writing Music

Write note head; attach stem. From G to B stems up on right side of note head;

from B to B stems down on left side of note head. Third line B stems up or down.

Write eight measures for the four open strings using whole notes. (1) Write the clef sign; (2) place the $\frac{4}{4}$ time signature; (3) Divide into measures by using bars, and place a double bar at the end.

Write eight measures for the four open strings using half notes.

Write a whole measure rest; half measure rest; quarter rest; repeat sign.

(1) Write the open string notes; (2) the 1st finger notes: (3) the 1st, 2nd and 3rd finger notes on the A string.

Review of Fundamentals

Music is written upon the ________

How many lines in the staff? ________

How many spaces? ________

Name the lines of the staff. ________

Name the spaces. ________

Can you name them in reverse order? ________

What is the proper name of this sign 𝄞? ________

What is the time signature? ________

What does the upper figure mean? ________

The lower figure? ________

Name three notes above the staff. ________

Name five notes below the staff. ________

Give the number and the name of each open string. ________

The whole rest is written above or below which line? ________

The half measure rest? ________

Music is divided into ________

What are bars? ________

What is the purpose of the double bar? ________

Describe the repeat sign. ________

Write the down bow sign. ________

Write the up bow sign. ________

LESSON 10

The 1st, 2nd and 3rd Finger on the D String

These tones on the D string are exactly opposite those learned on the A string in Lesson 9. F♯ and C♯ key signature of D major.

Hark! The Herald Angels Sing

Mendelssohn

LESSON 11

The Key of D Major: F♯ and C♯

A Key in music is a group of seven related tones; these seven related tones form the Major Scale.

The relationship of tones is the same in all major scales.

No. 1 is the scale of D Major: the Key Signature is two sharps, F♯ and C♯; there is a Whole Tone between each degree of the scale except the 3rd and 4th, and 7th and 8th degrees which are Half Tones (fingers close together).

Observe that the scale is divided into two equal parts of four tones each. After playing the first four tones on the D string lift the fingers carefully across to the A string where the next four tones will be found in exactly the same position.

The Scale of D Major

1.
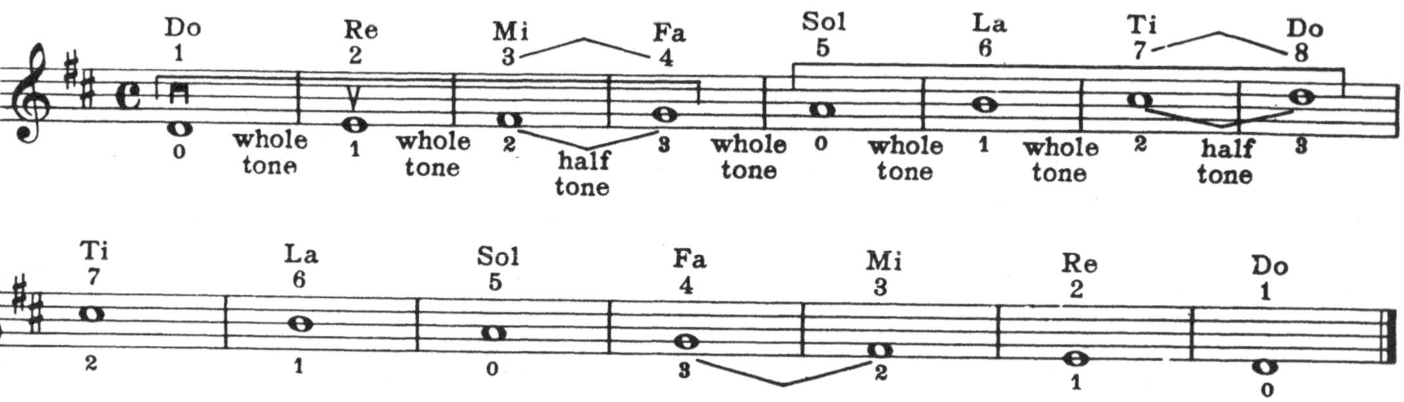

(a) detached
(b) two slurred
(c) four slurred

2.

3.
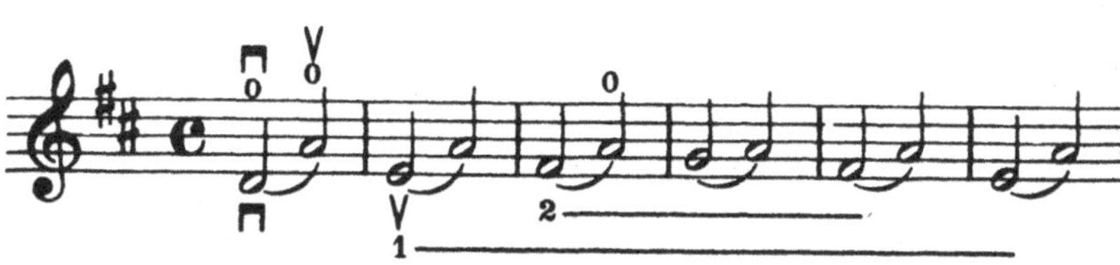

4.
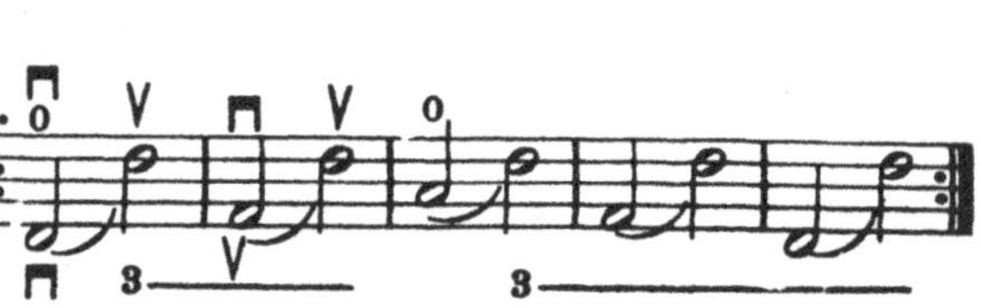

5.

6. 

7. 

Hippity Hop!

C.G.

8. 

Serious Thoughts

C.G.

9. 

LESSON 12

The Dot – Dotted Half Notes

A Dot placed to the right of a note equals one half the value of that note.

Dotted Half Note

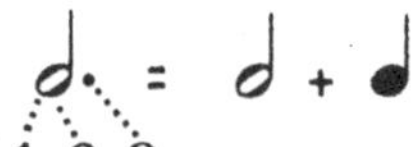

Count: 1 2 3

The Dot following a Half Note is equal to a Quarter Note and gets one full count.

Count: 1 2 3 1 2 3

Count: 1 2 3 4 1 2 3 4

Slowly on the down bow, faster on the up bow.

Count: 1 2 3 4

Smoothly Flowing

C.G.

Count: 1 2 3 4

The Glide Waltz

C. G.

6.

Valse La Grace

C.G.

7.

LESSON 13

The Dot – Dotted Quarter Notes

Dotted Quarter Note

In $\frac{2}{4}$, $\frac{3}{4}$ and $\frac{4}{4}$ Time the Dot following a quarter note is equal to an eight note. In Ex. 2 we see the way it is mostly used; the dotted quarter being followed by an eighth note completing the count of two.

That this important figure may be well understood Nos. 1 and 2 should be *la*-ed by the class while the teacher counts aloud.

Off for School

C. G.

German Folk Song

LESSON 14

Four Fingers on the A String

Diagram of the tones on the G, D, A, and E strings

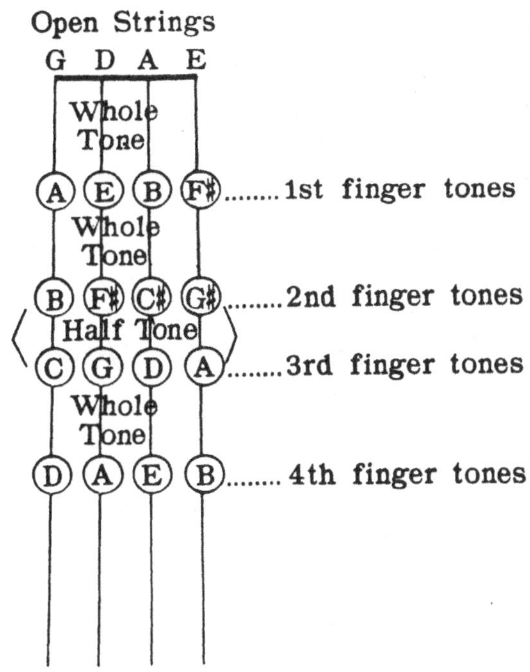

When crossing from one string to another take care to move the fingers straight across as the tones on each strings are in the same relative position.

Rules:

1. Keep the left hand straight.
2. Hold the fourth finger above the strings.
3. Do not reach forward or backward with the first finger.

The Key of A Major–Key Signature Three Sharps–F♯, C♯, G♯

1. 

2. 

(a) Detached

3. 

(b) Two Slurred

Toy March

C.G.

Air from the Ninth Symphony

Beethoven

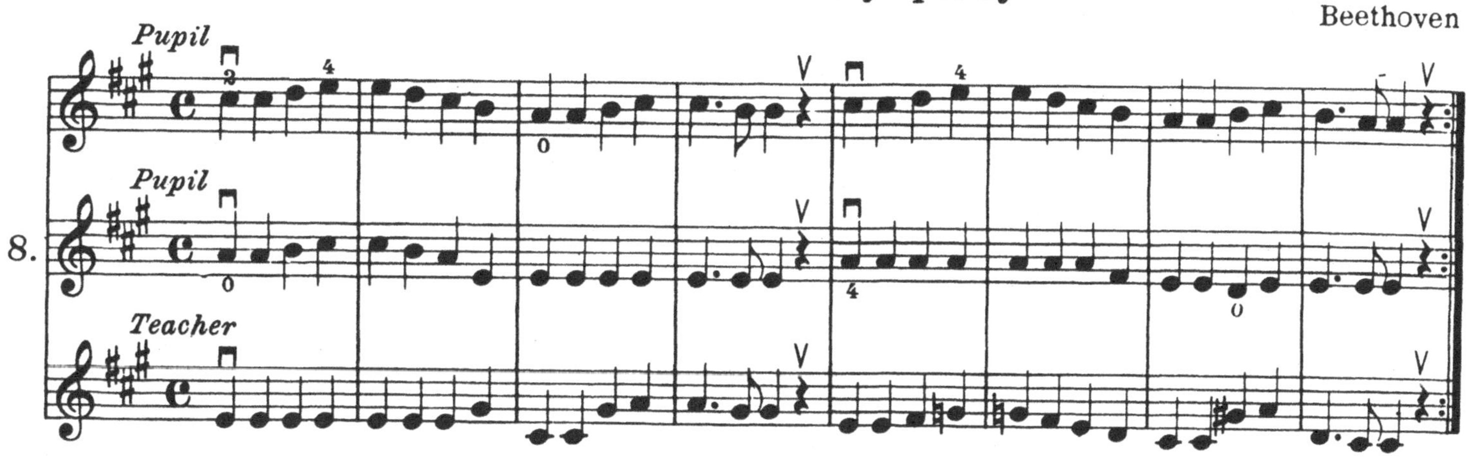

Four Fingers on the E String

The Key of E Major–Key Signature Four Sharps–F♯, C♯, G♯, D♯

1.
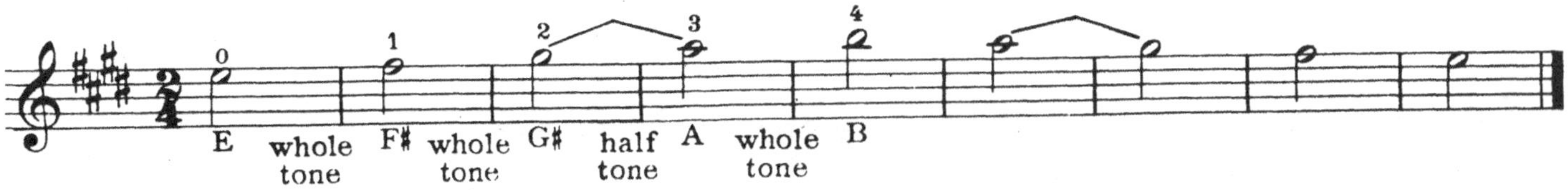

2.

3.

4.

5.

The Scale of A Major

Key Signature Three Sharps–F♯, C♯, G♯

6.

7. 8.

Whistling Jim

C. G.

9.

Still Waters

C. G.

10.

LESSON 16

The Unaccented or Up-Beat

A piece beginning on a weak or unaccented beat is said to begin on the Up-Beat. This pick-up note is usually played with an up bow.

The accents in music parallel the usage of language.

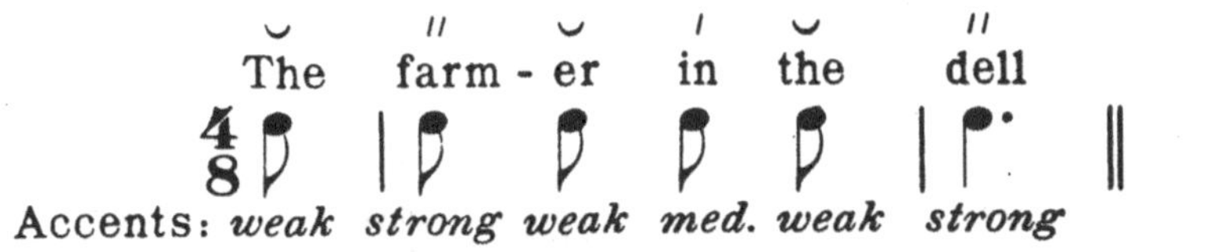

To give rhythmical balance the last measure will always be minus the amount of the up-beat, and the two will equal a full measure.

The Farmer in the Dell

Traditional

1.

German Folk Song

2.

English Folk Song

3.

My Bonnie

Scotch Song

4.

German Folk Song

5.

Highland Shepherd's Song

C. G.

6.

LESSON 17

The Staccato

The Staccato—a short, crisp tone played with little bow. The dots above or below the notes indicate they are to be played staccato; either singly or two or more in the same bow. Press lightly with the right forefinger, and stop the bow after each note without raising from the string. The time value of the notes shortened by staccato must be made up by an equal amount of rest.

1. 

2. 

3. 

A Short Theme

C.G.

4. 

The Shamrock Green

C. G.

5.

Long, Long Ago

Bayly

6.

For Written Work

1. D major scale

2. G major scale

3. A major scale

4. E major scale

Divide into measures.

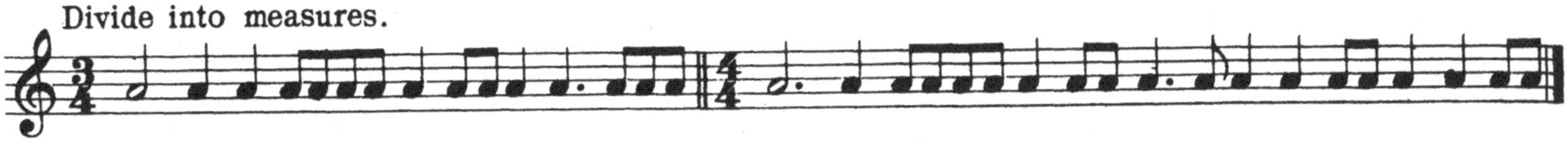

Every measure is wrong: correct by using dots.

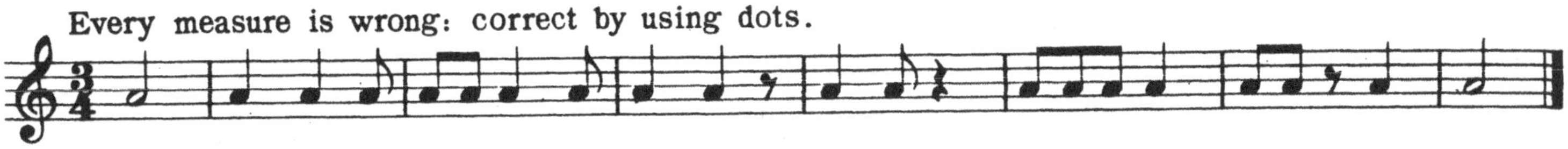

Every measure is wrong: correct by using notes.

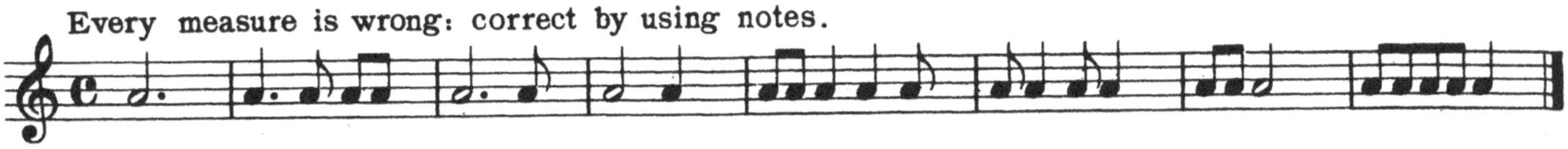

Every measure is wrong: correct by using rests.

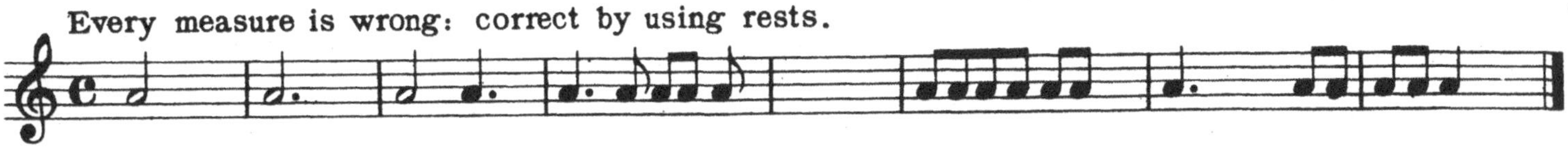

Review of Fundamentals

What is the key signature for G major? ______

What is the key signature for D major? ______

What is the key signature for A major? ______

What is the key signature for E major? ______

Between which steps of the major scale are the half steps? ______

How much does a dot add to the value of a note? ______

A dot following a half note equals? ______

A dot following a quarter note equals? ______

What is a slur? ______

What is a tie? ______

What sign is used for holding a note longer than the regular count? ______

The meaning of D. C. is ______

How are notes marked that are to be played staccato? ______

Name the notes played with the first finger on each string. ______

Name the notes played with the second finger on each string. ______

Name the notes played with the third finger on each string. ______

Name the notes played with the fourth finger on each string. ______

What are ledger lines? ______

Written work: on staves 1, 2, 3, 4 on blank music page.

Write the D major scale using half notes: remember (1) to write the clef sign; (2) the key signature; (3) the time signature; (4) divide the scale into measures; (5) write sharps before the notes that are sharped by the key signature; (6) mark the half steps.

Write the scales of G, A and E major in the same manner.

LESSON 18

Four Fingers on the G String

The Key of G Major–Key Signature One Sharp–F♯

1.

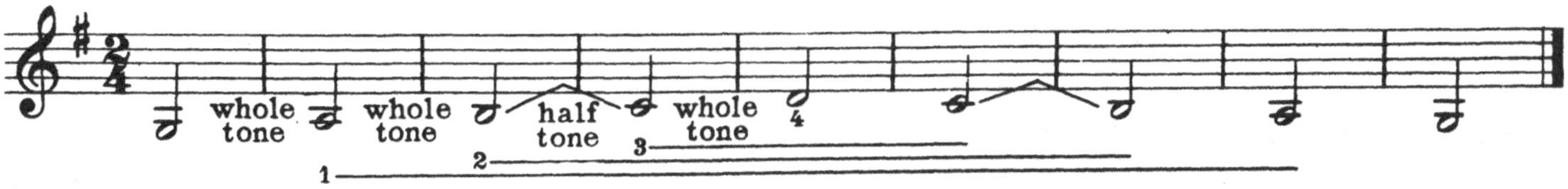

2.

3.

4.

Mary Had A Little Lamb

5.

The Scale of G Major

Nursery Song

6.

7.

Joy to the World

Melody by G. F. Handel

10.

LESSON 19

Loch Lomond

Scotch Folk Song

1.

The Minstrel Boy

Irish Air

2.

A Cloudy Day

Andante (moderate)

C. G.

3.

A Sunny Morning

Allegretto (brightly)

C.G.

4.

Air from the Beethoven Violin Concerto

5.

*Fermata or a Hold: this sign means to hold the note a little longer than the regular count.

LESSON 20

The After-beat

Notes that fall on weak and medium accented beats are called **After-beats**, and are usually played as an accompaniment to a melody.

LESSON 21a

Valse Debutante

Trio for three violins

C.G.

LESSON 21b

Our Class March

Quartet for four violins

C. G.

LESSON 22

To play well, the student should bear in mind the three T's of good violin playing: 1. Play in Tune; 2. Play in Time; 3. Play with a fine Tone.

Bowing Study

Practice this exercise with the five bowing examples above

Old Scotch Song

Moderato

Traditional

Fancy Free

Allegretto

C. G.

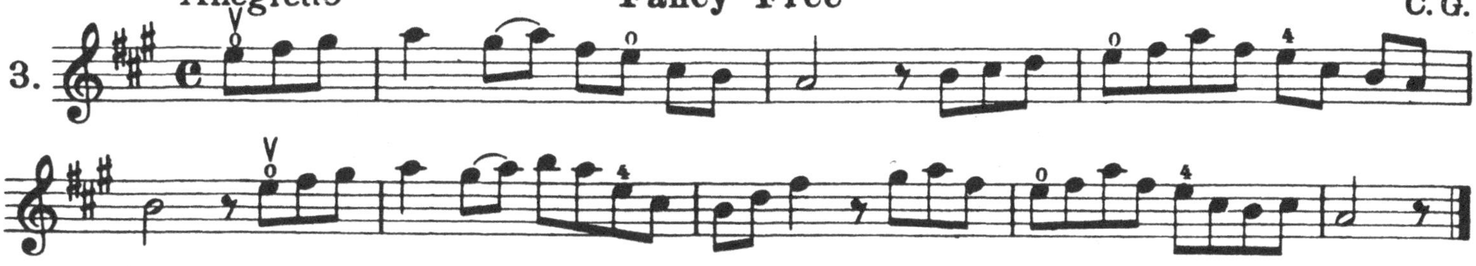

The First Mazurka

Allegretto

C. G.

LESSON 23

Joy to the World

Melody by G. F. Handel

LESSON 24

In Amsterdam There Dwelt A Maid

Old English Capstan Chanty
Arr. C. G.

LESSON 25

Characteristic

C.G.

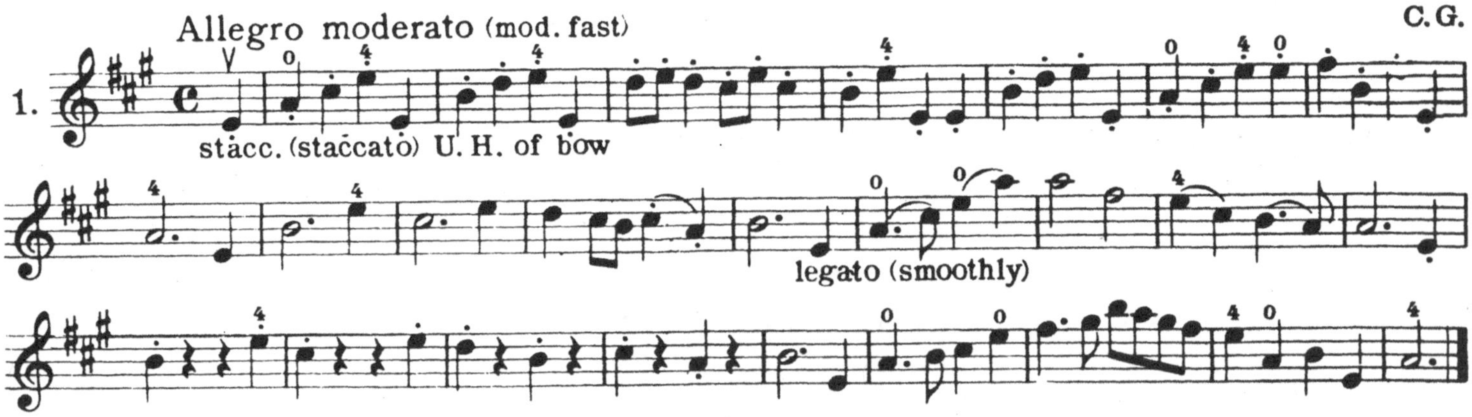

The First Ländler

C.G.

Zerkie's Capers

C.G.

Scouts On Parade

C. G.

I've Been Roaming

Old English Song

LESSON 26

The Harp That Once Thro' Tara's Halls

Old Irish Air
Arr. C. G.

LESSON 27

Old Bohemian Christmas Carol

Traditional
Arr. C.G.

LESSON 28

The Wearing of the Green

Irish Air
Arr. C.G.